motorsports

INDY CARS

Paul Mason

amicus
mankato, minnesota

Published by Amicus
P.O. Box 1329, Mankato, Minnesota 56002

Printed in the United States of America by
Bang Printing, Brainerd, Minnesota.

Published by arrangement with the Watts
Publishing Group Ltd., London.

Library of Congress Cataloging-in-Publication Data
Mason, Paul, 1968-
  Indy cars / by Paul Mason.
     p. cm. -- (Motorsports)
  Includes index.
  Summary: "Explains the history of Indy Car
racing and the how-to of the sport"--Provided by
publisher.
  ISBN 978-1-60753-118-0 (library binding)
  1. Indy cars--Juvenile literature. I. Title.
  TL236.M3543 2011
  796.72--dc22
                                    2009036922

Planning and production by
Tall Tree Limited
Editor: Rob Colson
Designer: Jonathan Vipond

Picture credits:
Getty Images: 3 (Gavin Lawrence), 6–7 and 27
(Jonathan Ferrey), 10 and 20 (Darrell Ingham), 11
(Torsten Blackwood/AFP), 16 top (Nick Laham), 16
bottom (Gavin Lawrence), 19 and 24 left (Robert
Laberge).
Dreamstime.com: 7, 22 and 23 (Lindsay
Baronoskie), 12–13, 15, 18, 24 right, 25 and front
cover bottom left and right (Sergei Bachlakov),
14–15, 21 and front cover top and bottom middle
(Todd Taulman), 16–17 and 26 (Leigh Warner).
iStockphoto: 13 (Scott Hirko).
QSC Audio Products: 8.
Corbis: 9 top and bottom (Bettmann).
Public domain: 29 top left (Drdisque), 29 middle
left and right (Daredevil), 29 bottom left
(Morio/GNU), 29 bottom right (David
Shankbone/GNU).
A.J. Foyt Racing: 29 top right.

Every attempt has been made to clear copyright.
Should there be any inadvertent omission, please
apply to the publisher for rectification.

1208
32010

9 8 7 6 5 4 3 2 1

CONTENTS

THE INDY CAR RACE

Imagine racing in an Indy car. Sweat pours down your face. Vibration from the engine blurs your vision. Your heart beats like a drum-and-bass track. The sideways force from cornering is five times that of gravity. But it's all worth it if you cross the line first!

OVALS AND STREETS

Indy car racing is famous for racetracks with high, banked turns at each end of long straights. These circuits suit cars with high top speeds. Some races are on street circuits with more twists and turns. These suit cars with good **handling** and **grip**.

TEAMS AND DRIVERS

Most Indy car teams have one or two drivers in each race. Each driver gets points according to where they finish. First place scores 50 points. Even coming in thirty-third scores you 10 points. At the end of the **season**, the driver with the most points is the champion.

▷ On fast oval circuits, such as Texas Motor Speedway, cars reach speeds of over 215 mph (350 km/h) on the straights.

TECHNICAL DATA

When they are moving at top speed, Indy cars travel slightly more than the length of a football field every second.

BUDDY RICE 15 DREYER & REINBOLD RACING

◁ The finish line at Indianapolis Motor Speedway is marked by the famous "Yard of Bricks."

WORLDWIDE APPEAL

Indy car racing attracts drivers (and fans) from around the world. Most champions have originated from the United States, but Sweden, Australia, Brazil, and Great Britain have also provided champions.

EARLY DAYS OF INDY CAR

"Indy car" was originally used to describe cars that raced at the Indianapolis Speedway. The banked "Indy" circuit is the most famous in America, and the Indy 500 race is one of the biggest motorsports events.

The Indianapolis 500-Mile Race is known to racing fans around the world as the Indy 500. It has run since 1911. That first year, almost all the drivers carried a mechanic with them, to keep one eye on the engine and another on the opposition.

▽ *The cars at the Indy 500 were known as "big cars," "championship cars," or "Indy cars." It was the Indy car name that stuck.*

TECHNICAL DATA

The first ever Indy 500, held in 1911, drew 80,200 spectators. Today, the race attracts 400,000 people every year.

The popularity of the Indy 500 soon led to similar races being held elsewhere. Many of the same drivers took part in these races as well. Eventually they began competing for an Indy car championship.

◁ The first Indy 500 was won by Ray Harroun in this car, called the Marmon Wasp.

BORN IN THE UNITED STATES

Indy car racing began in the United States but is now popular in many other parts of the world. In 2008, races were held in Japan, Canada, and Australia, but most of the races are still held somewhere in the United States.

▽ British driver Graham Hill celebrates winning the 1966 Indy 500.

BUILDING A WINNING CAR

The engine, chassis, and many other parts are the same on all Indy cars. Because the cars are so similar, the skill of the drivers and the work of the mechanics preparing the car are the only differences between teams. This makes for very close racing!

STANDARD CARS

All Indy car teams have to buy their engine and **chassis** from an approved supplier. In 2008, for example, every team used Honda engines, and almost all of them used a Dallara chassis. Firestone supplied all the tires.

▽ *The Andretti team, like every team, buys their engine from Honda. The engine is placed just behind the driver.*

△ During practice, teams try out the car using different kinds of tires— smooth tires, called slicks, for dry weather and grooved wet-weather tires (shown here).

A WINNING ADVANTAGE

Because all teams start with the same basic parts, the challenge is to get the best from these parts. Each team aims to **tune** the engine, **aerodynamics**, and suspension of the cars to suit their driver.

TECHNICAL DATA

The 3.5-liter engines of Indy cars produce more than 650 horsepower. That's over four times as much power as a typical family car.

ADAPTING THE CAR

When the driver is happy with the car, the team's work is still not finished. The car then has to be changed for every race, depending on whether it is on an oval track or a street circuit. For example, a car needs much greater braking power to compete on a twisting and turning street circuit.

BEHIND THE WHEEL

Imagine being behind the wheel of an Indy car. You have a mass of information and controls at your fingertips. Even the steering wheel is jammed with controls—so be careful where you rest your thumbs!

When the driver needs a drink, he or she can press a button to pump water into a hose leading into the helmet.

MAKING ADJUSTMENTS

Indy car drivers are able to make adjustments to their car as they race. For example, weight jacker buttons adjust the balance of the car from left to right, or right to left. Using them during the race, the driver can make changes to how the car steers and corners.

TECHNICAL DATA

- *During a race, the heart rate of an Indy car driver can peak at an incredible 200 beats per minute. This is as fast as the heart rate of a marathon runner or long-distance cyclist.*

- *A driver's body temperature can reach 102°F (39°C) while racing due to the warmth of the protective clothing combined with the car's vibration.*

▷ *Inside the cockpit of an Indy car, buttons, dials, and displays allow the driver to monitor and adjust the performance of the car.*

PERFORMANCE UPDATES

The driver constantly gets updates on how the car is performing. The temperature of the engine oil, coolant, and gearbox are all displayed. This warns the driver if the car is being worked too hard, or if there is a problem. A fuel readout lets the driver know how much fuel is being used and whether the car will make it to the end of the race. If there is plenty left, he or she may be able to push the speed a bit higher.

Gives extra power for overtaking

Allows the driver to talk to the team

Displays lap times, fuel **consumption** and oil, water, and gearbox temperatures

ACCELERATION AND BRAKING

Indy cars reach 60 mph (100 km/h) from a standing start in less than 3 seconds. On street circuits, they have to brake almost as hard as they accelerate. How on earth do they manage it?

▽ *Danica Patrick drives through turn 4 at the Indianapolis Motor Speedway.*

TECHNICAL DATA

At full speed, the pistons in an Indy car's engine pump up and down at a rate of 10,300 rpm (revolutions per minute).

BRAKING

Indy cars use different brakes depending on whether they are racing on street or banked circuits. On banked circuits, the cars can use lighter brakes. On street circuits, the brakes are about 30 percent more powerful, because the cars have to slow down much harder on the tight corners.

ENGINES

Every Indy car uses the same basic engine. Teams **lease** the engines from Honda. Honda provides engineers that travel to the races to help sort out any problems.

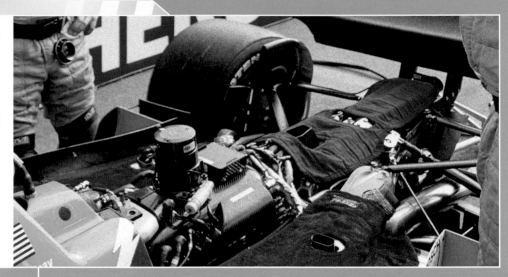

FUEL

Today, Indy cars are powered by burning a **biofuel** called ethanol. Burning ethanol contributes less to **global warming** than using other fuel, such as gasoline. Ethanol is also safer than gasoline because it does not burn as easily. It will be less likely to catch fire in a crash.

THE CAR: GRIP AND AERODYNAMICS

Indy cars generate so much grip at high speed that, in theory, they could drive along a ceiling—if you could find one long enough! This great grip is because the cars' tires and aerodynamics work so well.

AERODYNAMICS

An Indy car's aerodynamics (the way air flows over it) are adjusted to suit each racetrack. Where extra grip is needed, wings are adjusted so the airflow pushes the tires hard against the ground. If less grip is needed, the car is allowed to slice through the air more easily.

▲ On street circuits, cars need extra grip around tight corners, so the wings are set vertically to catch more air.

◀ On banked oval tracks, the wings are set horizontally for maximum speed.

TIRES AND SUSPENSION

If you folded a sheet of notebook paper in half and then in half again, the folded piece would be smaller than the **contact patch** of an Indy car tire. Despite this, the tires help the car grip the racetrack, even at well over 186 mph (300 km/h).

When racing, the **tread** of Indy car tires reaches about the same temperature as boiling water. The tread area is so hot and grippy that it becomes sticky, like tar.

An Indy car's suspension, which connects the body to the wheels, is designed to help the car to grip the track while cornering at high speed.

TECHNICAL DATA

At 155 mph (250 km/h), an Indy car's front tires go around 43 times every second. Before it is changed, a tire could go around as many as 60,000 times.

▽ *The Indy car's suspension absorbs bumps and keeps the tires gripping the track.*

RACE SAFETY

When Indy car drivers are racing at over 186 mph (300 km/h), accidents could cause terrible injuries. Fortunately, Indy car drivers are protected by some of the best safety measures in motorsports.

DRIVER SAFETY

If they are in a big crash, or their car catches fire, Indy car drivers have several layers of protection:

- Cockpits of Indy cars are designed to be crashproof.

- Drivers wear fireproof clothing and helmets. Even their helmet visors can resist fire for 45 seconds.

- HANS (Head And Neck Support) neck braces help to prevent terrible spinal injuries during a crash.

◁ The driver climbs into the cockpit wearing his firesuit and safety helmet. Underneath, he is wearing flame-resistant underwear.

△ *Milka Duno crashes at the Indy 500. The driver is kept safe in the strong cockpit, while the rest of the car absorbs the impact.*

TRACK SAFETY

Indy car racetracks are packed with features to make sure that if crashes do happen, they are not too serious:

- Special steel-and-foam barriers at oval racetracks absorb the impact of cars hitting them.

- **Run-off** areas on street circuits give cars a chance to slow down if they leave the track.

- Warning flags let the drivers know if there's a problem on the track.

- The trackside safety team includes paramedics, doctors, and firefighters.

TECHNICAL DATA

Every Indy Racing League race is attended by three paramedics, nine firefighters, two trauma doctors, and one safety coordinator.

RACE WEEKEND: QUALIFYING

Qualifying is a crucial time. Get it wrong and go slowest, and you start the race at the back of the **grid**—hardly anyone ever wins from there. But qualify the fastest, and you will get to start from the front.

STREET-CIRCUIT QUALIFYING

Street-circuit qualifying is very exciting. It takes place over three rounds:

Round 1: Two groups of cars race to decide the fastest six in each group.

Round 2: The 12 fastest cars then compete against each other to find the fastest six of that group.

Round 3: These final six cars compete in a 10-minute fastest-lap shootout to decide the top six starting order.

△ *Buddy Rice flies along the road during qualifying at the Honda Grand Prix, which is raced on the streets of St. Petersburg, Florida.*

TECHNICAL DATA

The Indy 500 is such a big, popular event that qualifying takes place over four days instead of one. It has its own qualifying rules, which are different from any other race.

OVAL-CIRCUIT QUALIFYING

First, the drivers draw lots to see what order they will go in. Then they do two warm-up laps, followed by four flat-out laps called green-flag laps. The **average** time of the green-flag laps is their qualifying time. The fastest qualifier starts at the front of the grid.

△ Hélio Castroneves powers around turn 4 on one of his four qualifying laps at the Indy 500.

RACE DAY

Race day is when all the hard work the drivers and their teams have put in is given its biggest test. During the next few hours of racing, they will find out if all their preparation and training is going to pay off.

WARM-UP LAPS

The race begins with the cars lined up in qualifying order. The racers then set off together on their warm-up laps. These are mainly to let the tires and brakes warm up so that they will have maximum grip when the race starts.

△ *The drivers take their places on the grid before the start of the Indy 500.*

RACE DISTANCE

Some Indy car races are as little as 200 miles (320 km) long. The longest, the Indy 500, lasts— unsurprisingly —500 miles (805 km). In all the races, the drivers have to balance going fast against making sure that the car lasts to the finish.

THE START

Indy car races start with a rolling start. After the warm-up laps have been completed, a green flag is waved as the cars cross the start line. The drivers put their foot down hard on the accelerator, hoping to improve on their qualifying position right away.

▷ *The cars speed through the first bend at the Bombardier Learjet 341 mile (550 km) race in Texas.*

TECHNICAL DATA

Indy cars can accelerate from 0 to 60 mph (0 to 100 km/h) nearly three times faster than the sports cars you see on roads, such as a Porsche 911.

IN THE PIT LANE

Indy car racing is very close, and the lead drivers are often separated only by seconds. The drivers have to make **pit stops** for fuel and new tires. A fast pit stop can help them overtake a rival— and a messed-up pit stop can cost victory.

THE PIT CREW

Each driver's pit crew is usually made up of 11 people, divided into two teams. One team jumps over the pit wall to the area where the car has pulled in. The second team helps from the other side of the wall.

◁ *The whole field comes in for a mass pit stop at the Indy 500 while a crashed car is cleared off the track.*

▽ All four tires are changed at the same time as the car is refueled.

TECHNICAL DATA

PIT STOP TIME LINE

00.00.00:	Car pulls in
00.00.50:	Car lifted by jack, fuel hose attached
00.01.00:	Tire changers start to remove tires
00.02.00:	Tires are removed
00.05.00:	New tires on
00.06.00:	Car dropped to ground
00.07.00:	Fuel hose removed
00.08.00:	Driver leaves pit stop

OVER THE PIT WALL

Six people go over the pit wall. Four tire changers wait ready, kneeling down, as the car comes in at 60 mph (100 km/h). The airjack operator lifts the car to make tire changes possible. A fueller attaches the fuel hose and fills the car's tank.

BEHIND THE PIT WALL

Five people help from the other side of the pit wall. The lollipop man signals when the driver should brake or go. Two tire assistants pass tires over the wall. Fire-extinguisher and fuel-hose operators stand by, ready to help if needed.

RACING STRATEGY

To win motor races of all kinds, you need a fast vehicle, a fast driver—and good strategy. You cannot win without knowing when to go fast, ease back, and take advantage of opportunities that come up during the race.

BASIC STRATEGY

The basic parts of a team's strategy are fuel use, tire wear, and speed. At full speed, drivers quickly wear out tires and use up fuel. If they go slow, the tires and fuel last longer—but they finish last. Getting the balance right wins races.

Danica Patrick became the first woman to win an Indy car race when the drivers ahead of her had to stop for fuel in the last few laps. Having judged her fuel consumption better, she was able to carry on past them to the finish.

▽ Whoops! A punctured tire won't do American driver Jimmy Vasser's strategy any good at all. He'll have to come in for a pit stop and lose race position.

DRAFTING

Drafting, or slipstreaming, is a way of getting a bit of help from another car. Moving cars make a little hole in the air. A second car, driving in this hole, or "draft," does not meet as much **air resistance**. Drafting gives cars extra speed for overtaking, and it can reduce fuel consumption.

△ *Hélio Castroneves leads the Indy 500. The drivers behind him save fuel as they draft the car in front.*

GLOSSARY

aerodynamics
Way in which air flows over an object.

air resistance
Amount of resistance or drag an object experiences as it moves through air.

average
Typical number in a group of numbers. To work out the average, you add all the numbers together and divide them by the amount of numbers.

biofuel
Fuel made from products that have been grown, for example sugar cane or corn.

chassis
Frame of a vehicle, to which the engine, suspension, and tires are attached.

consumption
Use or speed of use. High fuel consumption means using fuel quickly; low fuel consumption means using it more slowly.

contact patch
Part of a tire that is touching the ground.

global warming
Global warming is caused by human-made greenhouse gases that collect in the Earth's atmosphere and trap heat. Greenhouse gases occur naturally but are also released when fossil fuels such as gasoline are burned.

grid
Order in which vehicles line up at the start of a motor race. Usually they line up in rows of two, or sometimes three.

grip
Tire's attachment to the track. A lot of grip means a strong attachment, but low grip means the attachment is weak.

handling
Way in which a vehicle turns into and out of corners.

lease
Pay money to borrow.

pit stop
Stop made during a race to take on fuel, get new tires, and have adjustments made to the car's aerodynamics.

run-off
Area at the side of the track, usually on a corner, where cars are able to slow down to avoid a serious crash.

season
Period of time from the first race in the championship to the last.

tread
Grooves in a tire's surface that help it to grip.

tune
Make small adjustments to improve performance.

STAR DRIVERS

HÉLIO CASTRONEVES

Born: May 10, 1975
Nationality: Brazilian

One of the most popular drivers in Indy car, Castroneves is the youngest driver ever to win the Indy 500 two years in a row.

A.J. FOYT

Born: May 25, 1984
Nationality: American

Foyt's grandfather was a four-time winner of the Indy 500. In 2003, Foyt raced in his first Indy 500 at the age of just 19.

DARIO FRANCHITTI

Born: May 19, 1973
Nationality: British

A former junior karting champion, Franchitti was 2007 champion after winning the Indy 500 and three other races.

SAM HORNISH JR.

Born: July 2, 1979
Nationality: American

Hornish is the most successful Indy car driver of the modern era. He won the championship in 2001, 2002, and 2006.

TONY KANAAN

Born: December 31, 1974
Nationality: Brazilian

Kanaan set a record in 2004 when he became the only driver ever to finish every single lap of every single race.

DANICA PATRICK

Born: March 25, 1982
Nationality: American

In 2008, Patrick became the first ever female winner of an Indy car race, at the Indy Japan 300.

WEB SITES

www.indycar.com
An excellent web site, packed with information about Indy car, including the latest results, drivers, machines, and basic facts about the sport. There are fascinating statistics about the races and drivers past and present.

www.autosport.com
A one-stop shop for all motorsports fans, this is the place to go for up-to-date interviews with drivers, riders, team bosses, and just about anyone else involved in motorsports. The site carries news of Indy car, Formula One, MotoGP, and most other motorsports.

www.indycargarage.com
An online community for Indy car fans, this site also carries the latest news of races and other interesting stories.

www.indy500.com
The official website of the Indianapolis 500 race, with information on the event and its traditions, plus statistics and schedules.

INDEX